25
Most Treasured
GOSPEL HYMN
STORIES

KENNETH W. OSBECK

kregel
PUBLICATIONS

Grand Rapids, MI 49501

25 Most Treasured Gospel Hymn Stories

Copyright © 1999 by Kenneth W. Osbeck

Published by Kregel Publications, a division of Kregel, Inc., P.O. Box 2607, Grand Rapids, MI 49501. Kregel Publications provides trusted, biblical publications for Christian growth and service. Your comments and suggestions are valued.

Cover and book design: Nicholas G. Richardson

Library of Congress Cataloging-in-Publication Data
Osbeck, Kenneth W.
   25 most treasured gospel hymn stories / Kenneth W. Osbeck.
      p.   cm.
   1. Hymns, English—United States—History and criticism.
I. Title. II. Title: Twenty-five most treasured gospel hymn stories.
BV313.073   1999   264'.23'09—DC21   98-45851
                                      CIP

ISBN 0-8254-3430-0

Printed in the United States of America

2 3 / 04 03 02 01

CONTENTS

ABOUT THE AUTHOR

Throughout a long career of teaching and directing music, one of Ken Osbeck's prime objectives has been to lead Christians into a deeper understanding and appreciation of their church hymnal—next to the Bible itself, the most important book in one's relationship with God.

Since their retirement from teaching, Ken and his wife, Betty, have shared their dramatized hymn story and Bible character programs with more than five hundred church groups throughout the Midwest. God has greatly blessed this ministry and has made it a spiritually enriching time in the Osbecks' own lives. Ken and Betty were formerly teachers in the Grand Rapids area at the Grand Rapids School of the Bible and Music and the Grand Rapids Baptist College and Seminary (now merged as Cornerstone College and Grand Rapids Baptist Seminary)—Ken in church music and the fine arts and Betty in speech and drama. They both hold graduate degrees from the University of Michigan. Ken has also served as music director in seven area churches and for *Radio Bible Class, Children's Bible Hour,* and Youth for Christ. He is the author of a number of books for the church music ministry, all published by Kregel Publications. The Osbecks are members of Calvary Church, Grands Rapids, and have four grown children and two granddaughters.

PREFACE

Christianity is not a theory or speculation, but a life: not a philosophy of life, but a living presence. This realization can turn any gloom into a song.
—Samuel Taylor Coleridge

Prayer and praise can be compared to the two wings of a bird—both are absolutely essential if believers are to rise victoriously above the stressful circumstances of daily living.
—author unknown

What are gospel songs? When and where did they originate? How do they differ from the traditional liturgical hymns? Is gospel hymnody still relevant for today's contemporary church services?

Many Christian leaders have attempted to give a definition or description of this distinctive form of sacred music. Ira Sankey, often called the "father of the gospel song," once said: "These are songs that are calculated to awaken the careless, to melt the hardened, and to guide inquiring souls to Jesus Christ."

Another noted writer, Edmund S. Lorenz, in his book *Church Music: What a Minister Should Know About It,* defines a gospel song as:

a sacred folk song, free in form, emotional in character, devout in attitude, evangelistic in purpose and spirit. These hymns are subjective in their subject matter and develop a single thought, rather than a line of thought. That thought usually finds its supreme expression in the chorus or refrain, which binds the stanzas together in a very close unity, just as it does in lyrical poetry, where it is occasionally used.

In *Patterns of Protestant Church Music,* Robert M. Stevenson states that "gospel hymnody has the distinction of being America's most typical contribution to Christian song. Gospel hymnody has been a plough digging up pavemented minds. Its very obviousness has been its strength. It is the music of the people!"

Regardless of how one tries to describe or define the gospel song, it cannot be denied that these simply stated, heartfelt expressions have been used by God to advance His kingdom. Their simplicity and directness have a way of speaking to the most basic needs of humanity. They can be called "the language of the soul." Critics often disparage them for their poor literary and musical qualities—and many deserve such criticism. Yet gospel hymnody continues to be an effective influence in the proclamation of the "good news" as well as a mainstay of most evangelical church music ministries.

Gospel music is the product of a fervent revivalist spirit in America that began with the eighteenth-century Great Awakening. Several of the leading evangelists included Jonathan Edwards (1703–1758), with his convicting sermons such as "Sinners in the Hands of an Angry God"; George Whitefield, the English Methodist, who from 1738 to 1770 made seven trips to this country to conduct revival services throughout the colonies; and James McGready, a Presbyterian minister, whose preaching in the early nineteenth century stirred the southern states in outdoor services known as "camp meetings." Large crowds would gather, often after days of difficult travel, to live in their covered wagons or in temporary "brush arbor" camps.

A highlight of these happy gatherings was the group singing. The folksy, homespun songs became known as "camp meeting hymns." They usually expressed simple truths about personal salvation and the prospect of heaven. The tunes, often borrowed from the popular secular melodies of the day, were easily learned and sung from memory. These camp meeting songs generally had a catchy refrain that could generate mass enthusiasm, resulting in much foot tapping and hand clapping. The leader of the singing was the recognized "preacher with the loudest voice."

From these revival meetings came a large repertory of folk hymns and spiritual songs. Itinerant singing teachers and enterprising publishers compiled and commercialized these songs into popular hymnals such as *The Kentucky Harmony* of 1816, *The Southern Harmony* of 1833, and *The Sacred Harp* of 1844. An interesting feature of many of these books was the use of shaped notes to aid the singers in their sight reading.

About this time other sacred folk-style music appeared, including the African-American and the Appalachian Mountain spirituals. These, too, became an integral part of the American gospel song tradition. There was also another important revival stirring in the mid-nineteenth century among the established churches in the urban centers along the eastern seaboard. It was led by Charles G. Finney (1792–1875), a trained lawyer, an ordained Presbyterian minister, and later the president of Oberlin College. Finney's music associate, Thomas Hastings (1784–1872), composed numerous gospel hymns for these campaigns and compiled the first song book specifically intended for revival purposes. Hastings is recognized today as one who strongly influenced the development of evangelical church music.

The climax of the early gospel song movement occurred during the last quarter of the nineteenth century. It was centered in the ministries of Christian leaders like Dwight L. Moody (1837–1899), who conducted mass evangelistic crusades throughout the United States and in Great Britain. In 1866 this renowned evangelist also established the well-known Moody Bible Institute in Chicago, Illinois. One of the stated purposes of the school was to train young people for gospel music leadership.

Two other Americans also deserve special recognition: Ira D. Sankey (1840–1908) and Fanny J. Crosby (1820–1915). This trio—Moody, the magnetic evangelist; Sankey, the gifted musician; Crosby, the prolific writer—laid the foundations for the continued growth of the gospel song's influence throughout the evangelical community.

Following the Moody-Sankey-Crosby era, gospel music was dominated by the influence of the flamboyant evangelist Billy Sunday (1862–1935), who encouraged "sawdust trail conversions," and his genial song leader, Homer Rodeheaver (1880–1955). "Rody" introduced livelier and often more syncopated gospel songs ("Since Jesus Came into My Heart") with texts that continued to emphasize a very personal spiritual experience. Other important writers of this time include such musicians as Charles Gabriel, the Ackley brothers, and Virgil Brock.

The period from the close of World War II to the mid-1960s was marked by the rise of para-church organizations such as Youth for Christ, Campus Crusade, and the Billy Graham Evangelistic Association as well as the growth of the television medium. Appealing gospel music—songs, arrangements, choruses—again played a vital role in the spiritual success of these ministries as a means of attracting listeners and expressing personal faith.

From the mid-1960s to the present there has been an explosion of new gospel music, paralleling the rise of developments such as celebration-style (expressive) worship, the Charismatic Renewal Movement, the growth of mega-sized churches, and "seeker sensitive" services. These influences have resulted in a broad divergence of new musical styles—country, southern, rock, Christian rap, praise/Scripture songs—to complement the many innovative forms of church services that have been evolving. Today the publishing, recording, and performing of this contemporary music have given gospel songs an even greater role in evangelical ministries and have produced a huge commercial industry (e.g., the Gospel Music Association and the Christian Music Trade Association). There is, however, a growing concern among many evangelical leaders that the desire to gain a broader acceptance has watered down the biblical message and spiritual impact of much of this music. And too often the choice and use of music styles for worship services have become divisive issues in many congregations.

At a time when many worship leaders appear intent on discarding their hymnals and limiting their congregations to the singing of the latest "praise hits," *25 Most Treasured Gospel Hymn Stories* has been compiled. Its purpose is to ensure the preservation of a representative collection of proven favorites that are firmly rooted in the American gospel song tradition, that undeniably exalt the deity of Christ and the integrity of the Scriptures, that have significantly influenced the evangelical church music ministry, and that continue to lend themselves to meaningful and enthusiastic group singing.

Among older believers who have been spiritually nourished and sustained by this music, gospel hymnody will always have a cherished place in their affections. Many can recall some difficult experience from the past when a particular gospel song was used by the Holy Spirit to encourage and comfort their troubled souls. For the younger Christians, the periodic hearing and singing of these timeless gospel favorites should prove helpful in gaining an appreciative awareness of their evangelical heritage as well as providing a broader spiritual balance to the contemporary stylings presently enjoyed.

Finally, consider thoughtfully the following suggestions:

- Allow these gospel favorites to minister once again to you personally.
- Use them often for personal worship, family devotions, and church fellowship groups. Gospel singing—both in the home and in the church—can be an important part of every Christian gathering.
- Share a testimony regarding a favorite gospel song that has been especially helpful in your life.
- Reflect on the truths expressed as well as the circumstances involved that prompted the writing of these personal favorites.
- Resolve to raise your prayer and praise times to an even higher level than previously realized.

May we as God's people covenant together to leave for the next generation a worthy spiritual legacy of Christian songs and to respond more resolutely with King David, "the sweet singer of Israel":

I will praise God's name in song and glorify him with
thanksgiving. This will please
the LORD. . . .

—*Psalm 69:30-31*

ACKNOWLEDGMENTS

"Beyond the Sunset"/Virgil P. Brock/Blanche Kerr Brock/The
    Rodeheaver Co. (100%)/ASCAP
© 1936, renewed 1964 by The Rodeheaver Co.
    (a division of Word Music, Inc.)
All rights reserved. Used by permission.

"Great Is Thy Faithfulness"
Words: Thomas O. Chisolm
Music: William M. Runyan
© 1923. Renewal 1951 Hope Publishing Co., Carol Stream, IL 60188.
All rights reserved. Used by permission.

"My Home, Sweet Home"
by N. B. Vandall
© 1926 by Singspiration Music/ASCAP
All rights reserved. Reprinted by special permission of
    Brentwood-Benson Music Publishing, Inc.

"No One Ever Cared for Me Like Jesus"
by Charles F. Weigle
© 1932 by Singspiration Music/ASCAP
All rights reserved. Reprinted by special permission of
    Brentwood-Benson Music Publishing, Inc.

AMAZING GRACE
(MEDLEY)

*For it is by grace you have been saved, through faith–and
this not from yourselves, it is the gift of God–not by works,
so that no one can boast.*

–Ephesians 2:8-9

*I*n a small cemetery in a parish churchyard in Olney, England,
stands a granite tombstone with the following inscription: "John
Newton, clerk, once an infidel and libertine, a servant of slavers in Africa,
was, by the rich mercy of our Lord and Savior, Jesus Christ, preserved,
restored, pardoned, and appointed to preach the Faith he had long labored
to destroy."

Until the time of his death at the age of eighty-two, John Newton never
ceased to marvel at the grace of God that had so dramatically transformed
him from his early life as an African slave trader to a "proclaimer of the
glorious gospel of Christ." This was always the dominant theme of his
preaching and writing.

In 1779, assisted by his friend and classic literary writer, William Cowper,
Newton published a well-known collection titled *Olney Hymns Hymnal,*
one of the most important single contributions to the field of evangelical
hymnody. "Amazing Grace" was one of the nearly three hundred hymn texts
written by Newton for that collection.

Though the text comes from England, the tune is an early American folk
melody. It was known as a plantation song titled "Living Lambs." It was

first united with John Newton's text in 1831. The final stanza found in most hymnals, "When we've been there ten thousand years . . ." was added by an American, John P. Rees, and first appeared in 1859 in the *Sacred Harp* collection. "Amazing Grace" continues to be a favorite with God's people everywhere.

The text for "Grace Greater Than Our Sin" was written by Julia Johnson, who was a writer of Sunday school lesson materials for the David C. Cook Publishing Company. She also wrote approximately five hundred hymn texts, though this is the only one still in common usage. The composer, Daniel B. Towner, was for many years the director of the music department at Moody Bible Institute. "Grace Greater Than Our Sin" first appeared in Towner's collection, *Hymns Tried and True,* in 1911. Towner also composed such favorites as "At Calvary," "Anywhere with Jesus," "Saved by the Blood of the Crucified One," and "Trust and Obey."

I am in myself incapable of standing a single hour without continual fresh supplies of strength and grace from the fountainhead.

—*John Newton*

Amazing Grace

JOHN NEWTON, 1725–1807

American melody
From Carrell & Clayton's *Virginia Harmony*, 1831

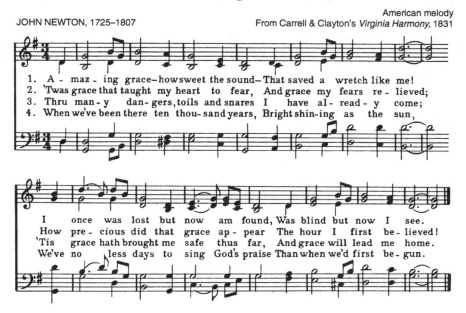

1. A - maz - ing grace–how sweet the sound–That saved a wretch like me!
2. 'Twas grace that taught my heart to fear, And grace my fears re - lieved;
3. Thru man - y dan - gers, toils and snares I have al - read - y come;
4. When we've been there ten thou - sand years, Bright shin - ing as the sun,

I once was lost but now am found, Was blind but now I see.
How pre - cious did that grace ap - pear The hour I first be - lieved!
'Tis grace hath brought me safe thus far, And grace will lead me home.
We've no less days to sing God's praise Than when we'd first be - gun.

Grace Greater Than Our Sin

JULIA H. JOHNSTON, 1849–1919

DANIEL B. TOWNER, 1850–1919

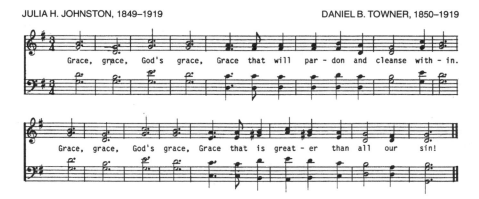

Grace, grace, God's grace, Grace that will par - don and cleanse with - in.

Grace, grace, God's grace, Grace that is great - er than all our sin!

BEYOND THE SUNSET
(MEDLEY)

*Now we see but a poor reflection as in a mirror; then we
shall see face to face. Now I know in part; then I shall
know fully, even as I am fully known.*
—1 Corinthians 13:12

*O*ur anticipation of heaven should shape our earthly activities—
encouraging us to live victoriously and joyfully regardless of life's daily
circumstances.

"Beyond the Sunset" is undoubtedly one of the best known and most
widely used songs about heaven in the entire field of gospel hymnody. Its
author, Virgil P. Brock, wrote more than five hundred gospel songs, most
of which were in collaboration with his first wife, Blanche. Several of these
songs still in use are "He's a Wonderful Savior to Me," "Resting in His Love,"
and "If You Could Know." After Blanche's death in 1958, a large monument
was erected in the Brocks' hometown at the Warsaw-Winona Lake Cemetery,
Winona Lake, Indiana, with the words and music of "Beyond the Sunset"
engraved in stone as a tribute to the ministry of this godly couple. Virgil
left the following account regarding the writing of this favorite:

The song was born during a conversation at the dinner table
one evening in 1936. We had been watching a very unusual
sunset at Winona Lake, Indiana, with a blind guest, my cousin
Horace Burr, and his wife Grace. A large area of the water

appeared ablaze with the glory of God, yet there were threatening storm clouds gathering overhead.

Our blind guest excitedly remarked: "I have never seen a more beautiful sunset."

I responded, "People are always amazed when you talk about seeing, Horace."

"I can see," he replied, "I see through other people's eyes, and I think I can see more clearly because I see beyond the sunset."

The phrase "beyond the sunset" and the inflection of his voice struck me so forcibly . . . I began singing the first few measures.

"That's beautiful," his wife interrupted. "Virgil, please go to the piano and sing that phrase again."

We went to the piano and soon completed the first verse. Then our guest urged, "Now you should try a verse about the storm clouds."

And the words for this verse came quickly as well. Recalling how for so many years our guests had walked hand in hand together due to his blindness, the third verse was soon added. Before the evening meal was finished, all four stanzas had been written and we sang the entire song together.

N. B. Vandall, a veteran gospel evangelist and singer, has composed a number of other favorite gospel songs that have been widely sung by Chrisians everywhere. Two of the most popular are "My Sins Are Gone" and "After."

Practice frequent thoughts about the eternal glories of heaven, especially when you feel yourself giving an undue amount of importance to the trivial events of daily living.

Beyond the Sunset

VIRGIL P. BROCK, 1887-1978

BLANCHE KERR BROCK, 1888–1958

1. Be - yond the sun - set, O bliss - ful morn - ing, When with our Sav - ior heav'n is be - gun;
2. Be - yond the sun - set no clouds will gath - er, No storms will threat-en, no fears an - noy;
3. Be - yond the sun - set a hand will guide me To God the Fa - ther, whom I a - dore;
4. Be - yond the sun - set, O glad re - un - ion, With our dear loved ones who've gone be - fore;

Earth's toil - ing end - ed, O glo - rious dawn - ing, Be - yond the sun-set, when day is done.
O day of glad - ness, O day un - end - ing, Be - yond the sun-set, e - ter-nal joy!
His glo - rious pres - ence, His words of wel - come, Will be my por - tion on that fair shore.
In that fair home - land we'll know no part - ing, Be - yond the sun-set, for - ev - more!

My Home Sweet Home

N. B. VANDALL, 1896–1970

N. B. V.

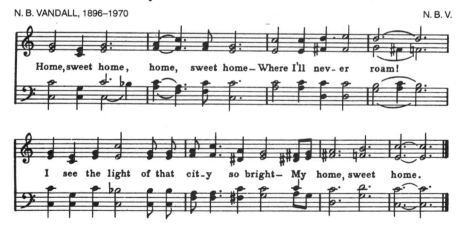

Home, sweet home, home, sweet home—Where I'll nev - er roam!

I see the light of that cit - y so bright— My home, sweet home.

BLESSED ASSURANCE

Let us draw near to God with a sincere heart in full
assurance of faith. . . . Let us hold unswervingly to the hope
we profess, for he who promised is faithful.
                                        —Hebrews 10:22-23

The Scriptures teach that we can know with absolute certainty that we have the life of God within us (1 John 5:13). This confidence is not based on inner feelings or outward signs. Rather, this "blessed assurance" is founded upon the promises of a faithful God and His inspired Word. It depends not on the amount of our faith but on the object of our faith—Christ Himself!

Though she became blind at six weeks of age through improper medical treatment, Fanny Crosby wrote more than eight thousand gospel song texts in her lifetime of ninety-five years. Her many favorites such as "Blessed Assurance" have been an important part of evangelical worship for the past century.

Often the themes for Fanny Crosby's texts were suggested by visiting ministers who wished to have a new song on a particular subject. As she once said, "Our home is a beehive of activity with so many friends dropping in and requesting a new hymn for some special occasion." At other times musician friends would first compose the music and then ask Fanny for matching words. Such was the prompting for the hymn "Blessed Assurance." One day Mrs. Joseph (Phoebe) Knapp, who was an amateur musician, the daughter of a noted Methodist evangelist, and a close personal friend, visited Fanny in her New York home.

"Oh, Fanny, I have had a new melody racing through my mind for some time now, and I just can't think of anything else. Let me play it for you and perhaps you can help me with the words."

After kneeling in prayer and clutching her little Bible, the blind poetess stood to her feet with face aglow: "Why, that music says, 'Blessed Assurance, Jesus is mine! O what a foretaste of glory divine . . .'"

Soon the words began to flow from her heart, and there was born another of the more than eight thousand gospel hymns by this godly woman, the "queen of gospel music." And still today our hearts are inspired and our spirits lifted as we sing this musical testimony together.

Only eternity will reveal fully the host of individuals whose lives have been spiritually changed and enriched through the texts of Fanny Jane Crosby's many hymns.

Beware of despairing about yourself. You are commanded to put your trust in God and not yourself.
–Augustine (354-430)

Blessed Assurance

FANNY J. CROSBY, 1820-1915

PHOEBE P. KNAPP, 1839–1908

1. Bless-ed as-sur-ance, Je-sus is mine! O what a fore-taste of glo-ry di-vine! Heir of sal-va-tion, pur-chase of God, Born of His Spir-it, washed in His blood.

2. Per-fect sub-mis-sion, per-fect de-light! Vi-sions of rap-ture now burst on my sight; An-gels de-scend-ing bring from a-bove Ech-oes of mer-cy, whis-pers of love.

3. Per-fect sub-mis-sion—all is at rest, I in my Sav-ior am hap-py and blest; Watch-ing and wait-ing, look-ing a-bove, Filled with His good-ness, lost in His love.

CHORUS

This is my sto-ry, this is my song, Prais-ing my Sav-ior all the day long; This is my sto-ry, this is my song, Prais-ing my Sav-ior all the day long.

BRETHREN, WE HAVE MET TO WORSHIP

Let us not give up meeting together, as some are in the
habit of doing, but let us encourage one another–and all
the more as you see the Day approaching.
–Hebrews 10:25

God is spirit, and his worshipers must worship in spirit
and in truth.
–John 4:24

The apostle Paul's favorite name for fellow believers was "brethren." He used this term at least sixty times throughout his various epistles. Paul's concept of the local church was a worshiping family—the family of God.

Worship is the cornerstone of a believer's spiritual life. The fundamental command of Scripture is that we are to love God with our whole being and to worship and serve only Him. The bedrock of the local church's ministry is its worship service. The manner of worship reflects the depth of our relationship with God—both individually and corporately.

But what is the proper way to worship? Many changes in worship services have occurred in recent times. Synthesizers, guitars, and drum sets have often replaced pianos and organs. Upbeat, repetitive praise choruses are replacing the traditional hymns and gospel songs. Drama, choreography, hand raising, and clapping are practices commonly associated with the more informal-contemporary "celebrations." Changes and practices such as these can be very disturbing to many older Christians, who have been spiritually nurtured on a more meditative type of service. Yet according to Scripture, there are just two basic requirements for true worship: (1) in spirit and (2) in truth. Differences based on cultural change and age preferences alone should never divide the family of faith. Each of us must learn to differentiate between unchanging biblical principles and variable cultural practices.

Regardless of our preferred styles of music and forms of worship, let us reaffirm our purpose each time we gather in our Lord's name to claim and to bask in His promised presence (Matt. 18:20):

- To truly glorify and "adore the Lord our God"
- To offer praise and gratitude for all of our spiritual provisions and material blessings
- To hear, learn, and respond to the inspired Scriptures
- To petition for our own needs as well as the concerns of others
- To ask and receive divine forgiveness for our sins
- To gain a greater desire to represent our Lord worthily in this needy world

---

It is in the process of being worshiped that God communicates His presence to people.

—C. S. Lewis

Brethren, We Have Met to Worship

GEORGE ATKINS, 19TH CENTURY

WILLIAM MOORE, 1825
in *Columbian Harmony*

1 Breth-ren, we have met to wor-ship, To a - dore the Lord and God;
2 *Let us love our God su - preme-ly, Let us love our broth-ers too;*

1 Will you pray with ex - pec - ta - tion As we preach the liv - ing Word?
2 *Let us pray and care for peo-ple 'Til God makes their lives a - new.*

1 All is vain un - less the Spir - it Of the Ho - ly One comes down;
2 *When at last we're called to heav - en, In His pre - sence we'll sit down;*

1 Breth-ren, pray, and God's great bless-ing Will be show-ered all a - round.
2 *And the Lord will then re - ward us Giv - ing us a heaven-ly crown.*

DEEPER AND DEEPER

I desire to do your will, O my God; your law is within my heart.

—Psalm 40:8

*I*nto the heart, the will, the cross, the joy, the love of Jesus—deeper and deeper I go. . . ." These beautifully worded lines with their soulful melody flowed from the heart of Oswald J. Smith after many difficult experiences during the early years of his ministry. He related in his book *The Story of My Life* that he was carried through these troublesome times by what he called his "morning watch."

> It was when I walked alone with God that I learned the lessons He would teach. I set aside a time and a place to meet Him, and I have never been disappointed.

Dr. Smith, regarded today as one of the finest missionary statesmen and evangelists of the twentieth century, described the inspiration that came to him for "Deeper and Deeper":

> Arriving in Woodstock, Ontario, I was invited to preach one Sunday morning in the largest Methodist Church in that city. As I walked along the street on my way to the church, the melody of this hymn sang itself into my heart and with it the words, "Into the heart of Jesus, deeper and deeper I go." I can still recall the joy and buoyancy of youth, the bright sunshine overhead, the thrill with which I looked forward to my service that Sunday

morning, as again and again I hummed over the words. I wondered if I could retain the music in my mind until the service was over. I was just twenty-one years of age. After preaching, I quickly returned to my rented room, and the first thing I did was to write out the melody as God had given it to me. I had been able to remember it, and it has never changed from that day to this. The writing of the remaining verses was much more difficult. It was three years later, in the First Presbyterian Church of South Chicago, which I pastored, that I completed them. It was then 1914, and I was twenty-four years old. The writing of the hymn afforded me much joy, nor has it ever grown old. I still love it and always will, for it was the child of my youth. It proves conclusively that God can impart His deepest truths to the hearts of the young, for I doubt I have ever written anything more profound since.

Evangelist Billy Graham, who spoke at Dr. Smith's funeral in 1986, paid him this tribute: "The name Oswald J. Smith symbolizes worldwide evangelism. His books have been used of the Holy Spirit to sear into the very depths of my soul and have had a tremendous influence on my personal life and ministry. He is the greatest combination of pastor, missionary, statesman, hymn writer, and evangelist of our time."

Alone, dear Lord, ah, yes! alone with Thee!
My aching heart at rest, my spirit free;
My sorrow gone, my burdens all forgotten,
When far away I soar alone with Thee.
                                        —Oswald J. Smith

Deeper and Deeper

OSWALD J. SMITH, 1890-1986

OSWALD J. SMITH, 1890-1986

1. In-to the heart of Je - sus Deep-er and deep - er I go,
2. In-to the will of Je - sus Deep-er and deep - er I go,
3. In-to the cross of Je - sus Deep-er and deep - er I go,
4. In-to the joy of Je - sus Deep-er and deep - er I go,
5. In-to the love of Je - sus Deep-er and deep - er I go,

Seek - ing to know the rea - son Why He should love me so—
Pray - ing for grace to fol - low, Seek-ing His way to know;
Fol - low-ing thru the gar - den, Fac - ing the dread - ed foe;
Ris - ing, with soul en - rap - tured, Far from the world be - low;
Prais-ing the One who brought me Out of my sin and woe;

Why He should stoop to lift me Up from the mir - y clay,
Bow - ing in full sur - ren - der Low at His bless - ed feet,
Drink-ing the cup of sor - row— Sob-bing with bro - ken heart,
Joy in the place of sor - row, Peace in the midst of pain,
And thru e - ter - nal a - ges Grate-ful - ly I shall sing,

Sav - ing my soul, mak-ing me whole, Tho I had wan-dered a - way.
Bid-ding Him take, break me and make, Till I am mold-ed and meet.
"O Sav - ior, help! dear Sav-ior, help! Grace for my weak-ness im - part."
Je - sus will give, Je - sus will give— He will up-hold and sus - tain.
"O how He loved! O how He loved! Je - sus, my Lord and my King!"

GREAT IS THY FAITHFULNESS

*Because of the LORD's great love we are not consumed, for
his compassions never fail. They are new every morning;
great is
your faithfulness.*
—Lamentations 3:22-23

One of the important lessons the children of Israel had to learn during their wilderness journey was that God's provision of manna for them was on a morning-by-morning basis. They could not survive on old manna, nor could it be stored for future use (Exod. 16:19–21).

While many enduring hymns are born out of a particular dramatic experience, "Great Is Thy Faithfulness" was simply the result of the author's "morning by morning" realization of God's personal faithfulness in his daily life. Shortly before his death in 1960, Thomas Chisholm wrote:

My income has never been large at any time due to impaired health in the earlier years which has followed me on until now. But I must not fail to record here the unfailing faithfulness of a covenant keeping God and that He has given me many wonderful displays of His providing care which have filled me with astonishing gratefulness.

In 1923, Chisholm sent his text to William Runyan, a well-known gospel musician and an editor with the Hope Publishing Company. Runyan was especially enthusiastic about this text and soon composed the appropriate music for it. He stated:

> This particular poem held such an appeal for me that I prayed earnestly that my tune might carry over its message in a worthy way; and the subsequent history of its use indicates that God answered my prayer.

From a humble beginning in the log cabin where he was raised in Franklin, Kentucky, and without the benefit of high school or advanced education, Thomas Obediah Chisholm became recognized as one of the important twentieth-century gospel hymn writers. He wrote more than twelve hundred poems, many of which appeared frequently in such religious periodicals as the *Sunday School Times, Moody Monthly,* and the *Alliance Weekly*. A number of these poems have since become prominent hymn texts, including such gospel favorites as "Living for Jesus," "O to Be Like Thee," and "He Was Wounded for Our Transgressions."

When we acknowledge God's goodness and faithfulness, we are able to offer Him praise regardless of the circumstances.

Great Is Thy Faithfulness

THOMAS O. CHISHOLM, 1866-1960

WILLIAM M. RUNYAN, 1870-1957

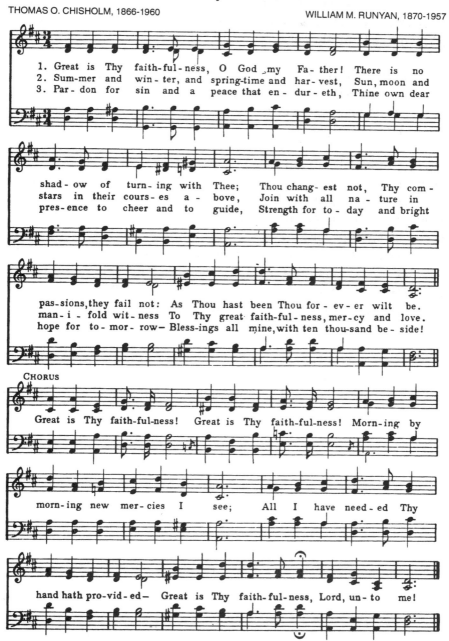

1. Great is Thy faith-ful-ness, O God my Fa-ther! There is no
2. Sum-mer and win-ter, and spring-time and har-vest, Sun, moon and
3. Par-don for sin and a peace that en-dur-eth, Thine own dear

shad-ow of turn-ing with Thee; Thou chang-est not, Thy com-
stars in their cours-es a-bove, Join with all na-ture in
pres-ence to cheer and to guide, Strength for to-day and bright

pas-sions, they fail not: As Thou hast been Thou for-ev-er wilt be.
man-i-fold wit-ness To Thy great faith-ful-ness, mer-cy and love.
hope for to-mor-row— Bless-ings all mine, with ten thou-sand be-side!

CHORUS

Great is Thy faith-ful-ness! Great is Thy faith-ful-ness! Morn-ing by

morn-ing new mer-cies I see; All I have need-ed Thy

hand hath pro-vid-ed— Great is Thy faith-ful-ness, Lord, un-to me!

HE LEADETH ME

He makes me lie down in green pastures,
he leads me beside quiet waters,
he restores my soul.

—Psalm 23:2-3

*B*ecoming a Christian is a thrilling experience—that time when one initially trusts in the redemptive work of Christ and becomes aware of a personal relationship with his Creator. Then there is also the glorious anticipation of spending an endless eternity with our Lord in heaven. But one of the joyous blessings of the Christian journey is simply to awaken each day realizing with childlike trust that our heavenly Father is guiding each step we take. And regardless of where life leads, "still 'tis God's hand that leadeth me."

Although the author of this gospel hymn, Joseph Henry Gilmore, was highly respected in his day in both religious and educational circles, today he is best remembered for this one gospel hymn hurriedly written when he was just twenty-eight years of age. He related this story:

> I had been speaking at the Wednesday evening service of the First Baptist Church in Philadelphia about the truths of the 23rd Psalm, and had been especially impressed with the blessedness of being led by God Himself. Later that evening, the wonder and blessedness of God's leading so grew upon me that I took out my pencil, wrote the text just as it stands today, handed it to my wife and thought no more of it.

Without her husband's knowledge, Mrs. Gilmore sent the quickly written text to the *Watchman and Reflector Magazine,* where it first appeared the following year. William Bradbury, the composer of the music, discovered Joseph Gilmore's text and wrote the fitting melody to match the words.

Three years later, in 1865, Joseph Gilmore went to Rochester, New York, as a candidate for pastor of the Second Baptist Church. He related:

> Upon entering the chapel I took up a hymnal, thinking, "I wonder what they sing here?"
>
> To my amazement the book opened up at "He Leadeth Me," and that was the first time I knew that my hurriedly written lines had found a place among the songs of the church.

When the First Baptist Church building of Philadelphia was demolished in 1926, it was replaced at the busy Broad and Arch intersection by a large new office building with a prominent bronze tablet containing the words for the first stanza of "He Leadeth Me." The inscription states: "This is in recognition of the beauty and fame of the beloved hymn, and in remembrance of its distinguished author."

Even in the details of life, recognize God's leading hand. Determine to trust Him more fully in the future.

He Leadeth Me

JOSEPH H. GILMORE, 1834-1918

WILLIAM B. BRADBURY, 1816-1968

1. He lead-eth me! O bless-ed thought! O words with heav'n-ly
2. Some-times 'mid scenes of deep-est gloom, Some-times where E - den's
3. Lord, I would clasp Thy hand in mine, Nor ev - er mur - mur
4. And when my task on earth is done, When by Thy grace the

com-fort fraught! What-e'er I do, wher-e'er I be, Still
bow-ers bloom, By wa-ters still, o'er trou-bled sea, Still
nor re-pine; Con-tent, what-ev-er lot I see, Since
vic-t'ry's won, E'en death's cold wave I will not flee, Since

CHORUS

'tis God's hand that lead-eth me.
'tis His hand that lead-eth me! He lead-eth me, He
'tis my God that lead-eth me!
God thru Jor-dan lead-eth me.

lead-eth me, By His own hand He lead-eth me; His faith-ful

fol-l'wer I would be, For by His hand He lead-eth me.

HIS EYE IS ON THE SPARROW

Are not two sparrows sold for a penny? Yet not one of them
will fall to the ground apart from the will of your Father.
And even the very hairs of your head are all numbered. So
don't be afraid; you are worth more than many sparrows.
—Matthew 10:29–31

*H*ow can I be discouraged when my heavenly Father watches
over each little sparrow, and I know He loves and cares for me?"
These words, spoken by a godly invalid woman to Mrs. Civilla Martin,
author of this text, were the inspiration that prompted the writing of this
favorite gospel song. Recalled Mrs. Martin:

> I wrote the song "His Eye Is on the Sparrow" in the company of
> a bedridden saint in the city of Elmira, New York. I was reading
> and singing to her and during our conversation, I chanced to
> ask her if she did not sometimes get discouraged. This is when
> she responded about God's care for the sparrow. Her answer
> prompted me to find paper and pencil, and in a very short time
> I had completed the poem.

Mrs. Martin was the wife of an evangelist/teacher/pastor, Dr. Walter S.
Martin. She wrote the "sparrow song" in 1904, along with another well-known
favorite, "God Will Take Care of You," which she did in collaboration with

her husband. Both of these gospel songs have enjoyed world-wide acceptance since that time.

The poem was sent to Charles Gabriel, one of the most prolific gospel song composers during the early twentieth century. Gabriel not only furnished the music for this text as well as a number of others, but he also wrote both words and music for many of his own songs, often using the pseudonym Charlotte G. Homer. Some of the Charles Gabriel songs still widely sung today include: "O That Will Be Glory," "He Lifted Me," "My Savior's Love," and "Send the Light."

It is interesting that our Lord chose the least valuable of all birds, the sparrow, to teach a profound truth. In God's eyes, no one is insignificant! He is vitally concerned with even the details of our lives; "The very hairs of your head are all numbered." The Bible also uses another bird to teach this inspiring truth: "Those who hope in the LORD . . . will soar on wings like eagles" (Isa. 40:31). With an awareness of God's concern for our lives and the promise of His enabling power to live victoriously, "Why should I feel discouraged?"

Make the truth of this Scripture passage your life's directive:

Though the fig tree does not bud and there are no grapes on the vines . . . yet I will rejoice in the LORD, I will be joyful in God my Savior.
—Habakkuk 3:17-18

His Eye Is on the Sparrow

MRS. C. D. MARTIN, 1869-1948

CHARLES GABRIEL, 1856-1932

1. Why should I feel dis-cour-aged, Why should the shad-ows come, Why should my heart be
2. "Let not your heart be troub-led," His ten-der word I hear, And rest-ing on His
3. When-ev-er I am temp-ted, When-ev-er clouds a-rise, When songs give place to

lone-ly And long for heav'n and home; When Je-sus is my por-tion, My con-stant Friend is
good-ness, I lose my doubts and fears; Tho by the path He lead-eth but one step I may
sigh-ing, When hope with-in me dies; I draw the clo-er to Him, From care He sets me

He: His eye is on the spar-row, And I know He watch-es me; His eye is on the spar-row, And I
see: His eye is on the spar-row, And I know He watch-es me; His eye is on the spar-row, And I
free; His eye is on the spar-row, And K know We watch-es me; His eye is on the spar-row, And I

CHORUS

know He watch-es me:
know He watch-es me.
know He watch-es me.

I sing be-cause I'm hap-py, I sing be-cause I'm free;

For His eye is on the spar-row, And I know He watch-es me.

I KNOW WHOM I HAVE BELIEVED

*I write these things to you who believe in the name
of the Son of God so that you may know that you
have eternal life.*

—1 John 5:13

There is much about the spiritual life we do not fully understand, but we can still live with certainty and triumphant faith. The apostle Paul understod when he exclaimed, "I know *whom* [not merely *what*] I have believed" (2 Tim. 1:12a).

Daniel Webster Whittle and James McGranahan, author and composer of this hymn, supplied many other choice gospel songs, including "There Shall Be Showers of Blessing," "The Banner of the Cross," and "Christ Liveth in Me." Whittle was a Civil War veteran who accompanied Union general William Sherman on his march through Georgia. At the close of the war Whittle was promoted to the rank of major and was thereafter known as Major Whittle. After the war he returned to Chicago, where he became treasurer of the Elgin Watch Company. In 1873, at the urging of D. L. Moody, the major left his successful position to become an evangelist. He enjoyed a most effective ministry for the rest of his life. He was ably assisted musically by P. P. Bliss and later James McGranahan. Many of Whittle's hymns bear the pseudonym "El Nathan." The piece "I Know Whom I Have Believed" is known by that name.

James McGranahan had a limited formal education, but at the age of nineteen he was teaching in singing schools throughout the East. He became known for his beautiful tenor voice and commanding personality. After Bliss died in 1877, McGranahan became music director for Major Whittle's evangelistic campaigns in England and North America. McGranahan was a pioneer in his use of male choruses. He collaborated with Ira Sankey and other musicians in many gospel publications. In addition to supplying the music for many of Major Whittle's texts, McGranahan composed the music for such gospel favorites as "My Redeemer," "Christ Returneth," "Christ Receiveth Sinful Men," "Verily, I Say unto You," and "Go Ye into All the World."

Note that the chorus of this testimonial song repeats the apostle Paul's statement to young Timothy: "For I know whom I have believed, and am persuaded that he is able to keep that which I have committed unto him against that day." (2 Tim. 1:12 AV). Make this Scripture a personal statement of faith. Another poet expressed the same confession this way:

My hope is built on nothing less
Than Jesus' blood and righteousness;
I dare not trust the sweetest frame,
But wholly lean on Jesus' name.
On Christ the solid rock I stand;
All other ground is sinking sand.

—Edward Mote

I Know Whom I Have Believed

DANIEL W. WHITTLE (EL NATHAN)

JAMES McGRANAHAN

1. I know not why God's won-drous grace To me He hath made known,
2. I know not how this sav - ing faith To me He did im - part,
3. I know not how the Spir - it moves, Con - vinc - ing men of sin,
4. I know not when my Lord may come, At night or noon-day fair,

Nor why, un - wor - thy, Christ in love Re-deemed me for His own.
Nor how be - liev - ing in His Word Wrought peace with-in my heart.
Re - veal - ing Je - sus through the Word, Cre - at - ing faith in Him.
Nor if I'll walk the vale with Him, Or "meet Him in the air."

CHORUS

But "I know whom I have be - liev - ed, and am per-suad-ed that He is

a - ble To keep that which I've com-mit-ted Un - to Him a-gainst that day."

IN THE GARDEN

Mary Magdalene went to the disciples with the news: "I have seen the Lord!" And she told them that he had said these things to her.

—John 20:18

One of the most dramatic scenes of Scripture is recorded in the twentieth chapter of John's gospel. Early on that first Sunday morning after Christ's crucifixion, while it was still dark, Mary Magdalene quietly made her way to the tomb. She was startled to find that the stone had been removed from the entrance. While standing by the empty tomb, she was amazed to hear the risen Lord gently call her name. One can well imagine the excitement in her voice when she responded, "Rabboni—my Master."

This thrilling biblical account became the basis for one of the most popular gospel songs ever written. The author and composer, C. Austin Miles, left the following account:

> One day in March, 1912, I was seated in the dark room where I kept my photographic equipment and organ. I drew my Bible toward me; it opened at my favorite chapter, John 20—whether by chance or inspiration let each reader decide. That meeting of Jesus and Mary had lost none of its power to charm. As I read it that day, I seemed to be part of the scene. I became a silent witness to that dramatic moment in Mary's life when she knelt before her Lord and cried, "Rabboni!"

My hands were resting on the Bible while I stared at the light blue wall. As the light faded, I seemed to be standing at the entrance of a garden, looking down a gently winding path, shaded by olive branches. A woman in white, with head bowed, hand clasping her throat as if to choke back her sobs, walked slowly into the shadows. It was Mary. As she came to the tomb upon which she placed her hand, she bent over to look in and hurried away.

John in flowing robe appeared, looking at the tomb; then came Peter, who entered the tomb, followed slowly by John.

As they departed, Mary reappeared; leaning her head upon her arm at the tomb, she wept. Turning herself, she saw Jesus standing; so did I. I knew it was He. She knelt before Him with arms outstretched and looking into His face cried, "Rabboni!"

I awakened in full light, gripping the Bible with muscles tense and nerves vibrating. Under the inspiration of this vision I wrote as quickly as the words could be formed and finished the poem as it has since appeared. That same evening I wrote the music.

So oft in the midst of sorrows, when hope seems cold and dead,
With lifted eyes, we too may see an empty tomb instead.
—author unknown

In the Garden

C. AUSTIN MILES, 1868-1946

C. AUSTIN MILES, 1868-1946

IT IS WELL WITH MY SOUL

God is our refuge and strength, an ever-present help in trouble.

–Psalm 46:1

This beloved gospel hymn text's author, Horatio Gates Spafford, had known peaceful and happy days as a successful young attorney in Chicago, Illinois. He was the father of four lovely daughters, a deeply spiritual and devoted student of the Scriptures, and a loyal supporter and friend of D. L. Moody and many of the other evangelical leaders of his day. Then he experienced a series of calamities, beginning with the Great Chicago Fire of 1871, which wiped out much of the family's real estate investments.

Two years later, when Moody and Ira Sankey left for Great Britain to conduct an evangelistic crusade, Spafford decided to lift the spirits of his family by taking them on a vacation to Europe. He also planned to assist with the Moody-Sankey meetings. Interestingly, it is reported that shortly before leaving, the family attended a service in Chicago where Moody was preaching. At that meeting all four Spafford girls made personal professions of Christ as Savior.

In November of 1873, at the time of the family's scheduled departure, Horatio was detained unexpectedly by some urgent business matters, but he sent his wife and four daughters as planned on the S. S. Ville du Havre, promising to join them shortly in Europe. Halfway across the Atlantic Ocean, the ship was struck by an English vessel and sank in twelve minutes. All four of the Spafford daughters—Tanetta, Maggie, Annie, and Bessie—were among the 226 passengers who drowned. Mrs. Spafford was one of the few who were miraculously rescued. As Horatio was busily packing, there was a knock at the door, and he was handed a cable which read simply: "Saved alone. Your wife."

Horatio Spafford spent hour after hour on the deck of the ship carrying him to rejoin his sorrowing wife in Cardiff, Wales. It is said that when the ship passed the approximate area where his precious daughters had drowned, Spafford received sustaining comfort from God that enabled him to respond, "When sorrows like sea billows roll—whatever my lot, Thou hast taught me to say, it is well with my soul."

Philip P. Bliss, a prolific writer of early gospel music, was so impressed with the experience and expression of Spafford's text that he soon composed the well-suited music. The hymn was first published in 1876 in one of the Sankey-Bliss hymnals, *Gospel Hymns Number Two*. It still ministers mightily.

Ask yourself if you can say with Horatio Spafford, "It is well with my soul," no matter what may be the circumstances that God allows.

It Is Well With My Soul

HORATIO G. SPAFFORD, 1828-1888

PHILIP P. BLISS, 1838-1876

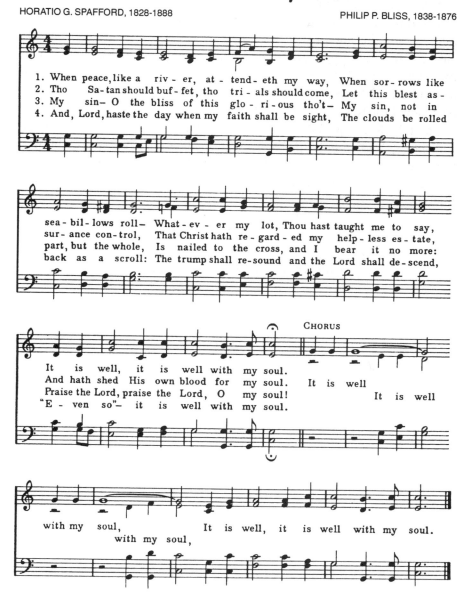

1. When peace, like a riv - er, at - tend - eth my way, When sor - rows like
2. Tho Sa - tan should buf - fet, tho tri - als should come, Let this blest as -
3. My sin— O the bliss of this glo - ri - ous tho't— My sin, not in
4. And, Lord, haste the day when my faith shall be sight, The clouds be rolled

sea - bil - lows roll— What - ev - er my lot, Thou hast taught me to say,
sur - ance con - trol, That Christ hath re - gard - ed my help - less es - tate,
part, but the whole, Is nailed to the cross, and I bear it no more:
back as a scroll: The trump shall re-sound and the Lord shall de-scend,

CHORUS

It is well, it is well with my soul.
And hath shed His own blood for my soul. It is well
Praise the Lord, praise the Lord, O my soul!
"E - ven so"— it is well with my soul.   It is well

with my soul,   It is well, it is well with my soul.
with my soul,

JESUS IS ALL THE WORLD TO ME

*I consider everything a loss compared to the surpassing
greatness of knowing Christ Jesus my Lord, for whose sake
I have lost all things. I consider them rubbish, that I may
gain Christ and be found in him.*
—Philippians 3:8-9

ill Lamartine Thompson was known as "the Bard of Ohio" for his respected literary and musical talents. He wrote many successful secular and sacred songs and he edited and published several collections. Biographical references comment that his greatest joy was writing and performing simple gospel songs. Thompson has provided hymnody with two enduring gospel favorites, the testimony for Christians, "Jesus Is All the World to Me," and "Softly and Tenderly Jesus Is Calling," an invitation song that has been influential in directing many nonbelievers to the Savior.

Thompson was educated at Mount Union College in Ohio and at the Boston Conservatory of Music. He also studied in Leipzig, Germany. He established the Will L. Thompson Company, a successful music publishing firm, with offices in East Liverpool, Ohio, and Chicago, Illinois.

The story is told of a visit that Thompson made to D. L. Moody's bedside as the noted evangelist lay dying. Because Moody was close to death visitors were being turned away, but when Moody heard that Will Thompson had called, he insisted upon seeing him. "Will," said Moody during this last conversation, "I would rather have written 'Softly and Tenderly

Jesus Is Calling,' than anything I have been able to do in my whole life." As the well-known evangelist entered his eternal rest, these words of invitation were again on his lips, words he had spoken and sung so often in his evangelistic campaigns: "Come home, ye who are weary, come home; earnestly, tenderly, Jesus is calling—calling, 'O sinner, come home!'"

And Thompson's words and music for "Jesus Is All the World to Me," published in his hymnal collection of 1904, have since been used by believers to express devotion to Christ and to testify to their dependency upon this heavenly Friend for all of life's needs.

All that I need He will always be,
All that I need till His face I see;
All that I need through eternity
—Jesus is all I need.
                                        —James Rowe

There are three essentials for a fulfilling life—(1) a faith to live
by, (2) a self to live with, and (3) a purpose to live for.
Jesus: "My life, my joy, my all."

The highest joy that can be known
By those who heavenward wend:
It is the Word of God to own,
And Christ to have as friend.
                                        —Andrew T. Frykman

Jesus Is All the World to Me

WILL L. THOMPSON

WILL L. THOMPSON

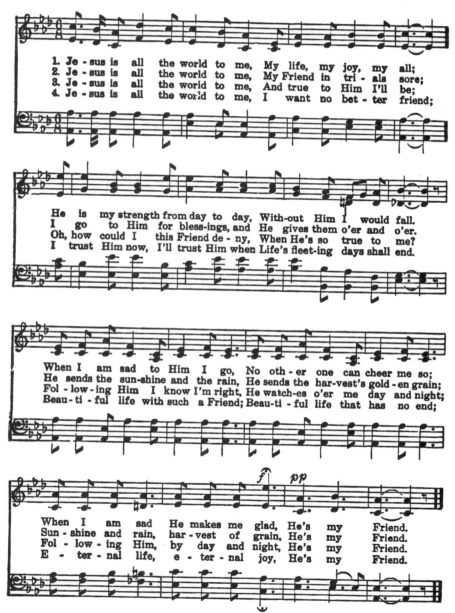

1. Je - sus is all the world to me, My life, my joy, my all;
2. Je - sus is all the world to me, My Friend in tri - als sore;
3. Je - sus is all the world to me, And true to Him I'll be;
4. Je - sus is all the world to me, I want no bet - ter friend;

He is my strength from day to day, With-out Him I would fall.
I go to Him for bless-ings, and He gives them o'er and o'er.
Oh, how could I this Friend de - ny, When He's so true to me?
I trust Him now, I'll trust Him when Life's fleet-ing days shall end.

When I am sad to Him I go, No oth - er one can cheer me so;
He sends the sun-shine and the rain, He sends the har-vest's gold - en grain;
Fol - low-ing Him I know I'm right, He watch-es o'er me day and night;
Beau-ti - ful life with such a Friend; Beau-ti - ful life that has no end;

When I am sad He makes me glad, He's my Friend.
Sun - shine and rain, har - vest of grain, He's my Friend.
Fol - low - ing Him, by day and night, He's my Friend.
E - ter - nal life, e - ter - nal joy, He's my Friend.

MY REDEEMER

I will sing unto the LORD as long as I live: I will sing praise
to my God while I have my being. My meditation of him
shall be sweet: I will be glad in the LORD.
—Psalm 104:33–34 KJV

*M*any of our finest gospel hymns have been born out of some tragic experience or event. "My Redeemer," though expressing a joyful note of praise, was found in the wreckage of a train accident which had just claimed the life of its author, P. P. Bliss, a noted contributor to early gospel music.

At the age of thirty-eight and at the very height of his fruitful musical ministry, Philip Paul Bliss's life ended suddenly in tragedy.

During the Christmas season of 1876, Bliss and his wife had visited his mother at his childhood home in Rome, Pennsylvania. As they were returning by train to Chicago to assist in an evangelistic crusade, a railroad bridge near Ashtabula, Ohio, collapsed. Their train plunged into a ravine sixty feet below and caught fire. One hundred passengers perished miserably.

Bliss somehow survived the fall and escaped through a window. However, as he frantically searched through the wreckage in an attempt to rescue his wife, he too perished with her in the fire. Neither body was ever recovered. Quite miraculously, however, among Bliss's belongings in the train wreckage was a manuscript on which he evidently had been working. The hymn text just finished was "My Redeemer."

The shocking report of Bliss's fatal accident made a profound impact on evangelical Christians everywhere. Upon hearing the news, two of Bliss's personal friends, composer James McGranahan and evangelist Major Daniel Whittle, left separately for the site of the accident, each hoping to find some trace of the body of their mutually esteemed friend. As he moved about in the large crowd, McGranahan recognized the major, though they had never met. The major, too, had heard previous accounts from Bliss about the talented James McGranahan and how this man should be in full-time Christian service. The major challenged McGranahan "to continue the work that our dear friend Philip has begun." McGranahan took the manuscript of Bliss's new hymn text that Major Whittle had found in a trunk and promised to prayerfully consider this challenge.

At their first public rally together following the accident, the hymn "My Redeemer" was introduced. The large Chicago audience was told that Major Whittle had found the text among Bliss's belongings and that James McGranahan had just recently composed the music for Philip P. Bliss's final words: "He from death to life hath brought me, Son of God, with Him to be." One can imagine the emotion that accompanied the singing at that service.

Renew your resolve to live each remaining day by singing
praise to God, meditating on Him, and being glad in the Lord.

My Redeemer

PHILIP P. BLISS, 1838-1876

JAMES McGRANAHAN, 1840-1907

1. I will sing of my Re-deem-er And His won-drous love to me;
2. I will tell the won-drous sto-ry, How, my lost es-tate to save,
3. I will praise my dear Re-deem-er, His tri-um-phant pow'r I'll tell.
4. I will sing of my Re-deem-er And His heav'n-ly love to me;

On the cru-el cross He suf-fered, From the curse to set me free.
In His bound-less love and mer-cy, He the ran-som free-ly gave.
How the vic-to-ry He giv-eth O-ver sin and death and hell.
He from death to life hath bro't me, Son of God with Him to be.

CHORUS

Sing, O sing of my Re-deem-er,
of my Re-deem-er, Sing, O sing of my Re-deem-er,

With His blood He pur-chased me;
He pur-chased me, With His blood He pur-chased me;

On the cross He sealed my par-don,
He sealed my par-don, On the cross He sealed my par-don,

Paid the debt and made me free.
and made me free, and made me free.

Number 14

MY SAVIOR'S LOVE

*Live a life of love, just as Christ loved us and gave himself
up for us as a fragrant offering and sacrifice to God.*
—Ephesians 5:2

ove is the foundation for the entire Christian faith. God's basic attribute is love (1 John 4:8). The Father supplied a model of sacrificial love by providing salvation for man through the atoning work of Christ. Then He gave us the indwelling Holy Spirit so that we could respond to Him and seek to imitate His love in service to others.

Historians have noted that the ancient Greeks expressed three levels of love: *Eros*—a "give me" kind of love; *Philia*—a "give and take" kind of love—"You love me and I'll love you"; and *Agape*—an unconditional kind of love—"I love you simply for who you are."

Our Savior's love was *agape* love in its highest form. He loved us enough to suffer humiliation and death for a world of rebellious sinners. Only when we are gathered "with the ransomed in glory" will we know fully the meaning of this divine love. In the meantime, however, the scriptural command is that we are to live a life of love that ministers to the needs of others as a "fragrant offering and sacrifice to God."

Charles Hutchinson Gabriel, author and composer of "My Savior's Love," was the most prolific and popular gospel song composer during the height of the Billy Sunday-Homer Rodeheaver evangelistic crusades. He edited more than forty hymnals and helped publish more than eight thousand gospel songs throughout his lifetime. In 1912, Gabriel joined the

Rodeheaver-Hall-Mack Music Company as its editor and maintained this position until his death in 1932.

Charles H. Gabriel generally wrote both the words and music for his songs, often using the pseudonym of Charlotte G. Homer. Other well-known gospel songs by this gifted man include "Since Jesus Came into My Heart," "He Is So Precious to Me," "He Lifted Me," "O That Will Be Glory for Me," "Send the Light," and "Higher Ground."

"My Savior's Love" first appeared in 1905 in the hymnal *Praises,* compiled and published by another fine gospel musician of that era, E. O. Excell. It is still a favorite with God's people.

All my theology is reduced to this narrow
compass—Christ Jesus came into this world
to save sinners!
—Archibald Alexander

My Savior's Love

CHARLES H. GABRIEL, 1856-1932

CHARLES H. GABRIEL, 1856-1932

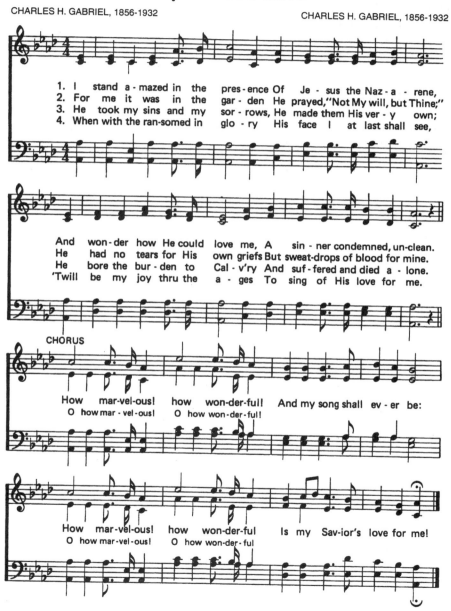

1. I stand a-mazed in the pres-ence Of Je-sus the Naz-a-rene,
2. For me it was in the gar-den He prayed, "Not My will, but Thine;"
3. He took my sins and my sor-rows, He made them His ver-y own;
4. When with the ran-somed in glo-ry His face I at last shall see,

And won-der how He could love me, A sin-ner condemned, un-clean.
He had no tears for His own griefs But sweat-drops of blood for mine.
He bore the bur-den to Cal-v'ry And suf-fered and died a-lone.
'Twill be my joy thru the a-ges To sing of His love for me.

CHORUS

How mar-vel-ous! how won-der-ful! And my song shall ev-er be:
O how mar-vel-ous! O how won-der-ful!

How mar-vel-ous! how won-der-ful Is my Sav-ior's love for me!
O how mar-vel-ous! O how won-der-ful

NEAR TO THE HEART
OF GOD

Submit yourselves, then, to God. Resist the devil, and he
will flee from you. Come near to God and he will come
near to you.

—James 4:7-8

*A*n effective gospel song can be described as a "spiritual experience that is born in the soul of one individual and in turn continues to minister to the heartfelt needs of others." This devotional hymn,
"Near to the Heart of God," is an excellent example of that truth. It was
written in 1901 by a distinguished Presbyterian minister, Cleland Boyd
McAfee, after he received the tragic news that diphtheria had just claimed
the lives of his two beloved nieces. Stunned and shaken, Pastor McAfee
turned to God and the Scriptures. Soon the words and music for this hymn
began to flow from his grieving heart.

Several days later, during the time of the double funeral, McAfee sang
the new hymn for his bereaved brother and sister-in-law, parents of the
two girls. On the following Sunday, Dr. McAfee's church choir repeated
their pastor's new song as a Communion hymn at the worship service. "Near
to the Heart of God" soon became widely used to minister comfort and
spiritual healing to God's people everywhere.

Though Dr. Cleland McAfee became well known as an eminent
theologian, a brilliant speaker, the author of numerous books, and a
moderator in his denomination, today he is no doubt best remembered

for this tender devotional hymn, written during a time of deep personal sorrow. Its ministry to hurting hearts still continues.

The hymnal can be a source of much comfort when we are facing a difficult situation. Through the centuries Christians have been drawn closer to God by sharing in the spiritual expressions of others whose emotional and physical struggles have prompted the writing of our enduring hymns.

But of even greater importance is God's inspired Word itself, where we find His eternal promises and sustaining strength in passages such as these:

> *The LORD is close to the brokenhearted and saves those who are crushed in spirit.*
> *—Psalm 34:18*

> *When anxiety was great within me, your consolation brought joy to my soul.*
> *—Psalm 94:19*

God does not provide comfort for us in our need merely that we might remain comfortable. Rather, He desires that we in turn might learn to comfort and encourage others in their times of stress to "provide for those who grieve . . . a garment of praise instead of a spirit of despair" (Isa. 61:3).

Near to the Heart of God

CLELAND B. McAFEE, 1866-1944

CLELAND B. McAFEE, 1866-1944

1 There is a place of qui - et rest, Near to the heart of God;
2 *There is a place of com-fort sweet, Near to the heart of God;*
3 There is a place of full re - lease, Near to the heart of God;

1 A place where sin can - not mo-lest, Near to the heart of God.
2 *A place where we our Sav - ior meet, Near to the heart of God.*
3 A place where all is joy and peace, Near to the heart of God.

O Je - sus, blest Re - deem - er, Sent from the heart of God,

Hold us, who wait be - fore Thee, Near to the heart of God.

NO ONE EVER CARED
FOR ME LIKE JESUS

Where is God my Maker, who gives
songs in the night?

–*Job 35:10*

It is not difficult to sing songs of praise when all is well. Often, however, God gives a special song to His hurting children during the "nighttimes" of life. Believers find new joys in their seasons of sorrow and despair, and they discover a greater closeness with their Lord during times of deep need. The apostle John wrote the Book of Revelation while on the barren island of Patmos; John Bunyan completed the classic *Pilgrim's Progress* while in the Bedford jail; and Fanny Crosby once remarked, "If I had not lost my sight, I could never have written all the hymns God gave me."

Charles Weigle's song "No One Ever Cared for Me Like Jesus" was the result of one of the darkest periods of his life. Weigle spent most of his years as an itinerant evangelist and gospel songwriter of more than four hundred songs. One day after returning home from an evangelistic crusade, he found a note left by his wife of many years. It said, "Charlie, I've been a fool. I've done without a lot of things long enough. From here on out, I'm getting all I can of what the world owes me. I know you'll continue to be a fool for Jesus, but for me—it's good-bye!"

Weigle said that he became so despondent during the next several years that there were times when he even contemplated suicide. Filled with terrible despair, he felt that no one really cared for him anymore. Gradually, however, his spiritual faith was restored, and he once again became active in the Christian ministry.

Weigle related:

> One day I received the sad news that my wife had died and under very heartbreaking and tragic circumstances. She had had less than five years in which to "try the world" and eternity had begun for her. And what did the future hold for me? It was while reviewing the heartrending experiences of the past few years and reflecting upon the goodness and love of the Savior, who never forsook me through it all, that there was rekindled in my soul the desire to write a song. This song would be a summation of my whole life experience with this wonderful friend. It was a story the whole world needed to know and it came to me as fast as I could put it down. It was the first song I had written since the day my world seemed to fall apart. Now I wanted the whole wide world to know that "No One Ever Cared for Me Like Jesus."

From a heart that had been broken and graciously restored by God came the words and music of this gospel song favorite.

With God's help, determine to rise above the hurts you may be experiencing and to turn them into expressions of praise.

No One Ever Cared for Me Like Jesus

CHARLES F. WEIGLE, 1871-1966

C. F. W.

1. I would love to tell you what I think of Je - sus, Since I found in
2. All my life was full of sin when Je - sus found me, All my heart was
3. Ev - 'ry day He comes to me with new as - sur - ance, More and more I

Him a friend so strong and true; I would tell you how He changed my life com -
full of mis - er - y and woe; Je - sus placed His strong and lov - ing arms a -
un - der - stand His words of love; But I'll nev - er know just why He came to

Refrain

plete - ly, He did some-thing that no oth - er friend could do.
bout me, And He led me in the way I ought to go. No one ev-er
save me, Till some day I see His bless-ed face a - bove.

cared for me like Je - sus, There's no oth - er friend so kind as He, No one

else could take the sin and dark-ness from me, O how much He cared for me.

SAVED BY GRACE

And I—in righteousness I will see your face; when I awake,
I will be satisfied with seeing your likeness.
—Psalm 17:15

The Bible states boldly that we are all sinners in the sight of God. But it also assures us that we were created in His image—and we are so important to Him that He sent His Son to redeem us and to restore our fellowship with Him. To receive this gift of grace means that we have been saved from eternal damnation and given the promise of one day seeing our Savior "face to face."

Fanny Crosby, the blind poetess, often expressed her fondness for Alfred Tennyson's final poem, "Crossing the Bar," and especially the line "I hope to see my Pilot face to face." The anticipation of seeing Christ was always the dominant theme of her life. She was further inspired to write "Saved by Grace" by the final words spoken by a pastor friend on his deathbed: "If each of us is faithful to the grace which is given to us by Christ, that same grace which teaches us how to live will also teach us how to die."

With a sense of divine inspiration, Fanny Crosby completed the new lines in a matter of minutes. She titled the poem "Some Day" and often referred to it as her "heart song." She sent it to her publisher, the Biglow-Main Company, and shortly received her customary two-dollar check.

Several years later Ira Sankey saw the poem in print and asked George Stebbins, a noted composer of early gospel music, to furnish the music for Fanny's text. Stebbins completed the appropriate music and also added the chorus to the four stanzas.

"Saved by Grace" soon became one of the personal favorites of both Dwight L. Moody and Ira Sankey during the latter period of their evangelistic ministry. They used the song at nearly every service. It was stated that whenever this song was sung at one of these meetings, a typical scene was the sight of "old Moody" sitting on the platform with a far-off look in his eyes while the tears flowed freely down his ruddy, whiskered cheeks. It is also reported that on the morning of August 13, 1908, Ira Sankey drifted off into a final coma singing Fanny Crosby's "heart song."

George Cole Stebbins is another influential name in the development of the early gospel song movement. He became closely associated with leading evangelists like D. L. Moody, George F. Pentecost, and Major Daniel Whittle. He is also the composer of such well-known gospel hymns as "Ye Must Be Born Again," "There Is a Green Hill Far Away," and "Jesus, I Come."

Raise your voice in praise to Christ for His redeeming grace
which has made possible the glorious prospect of someday
seeing Him "face to face."

Saved by Grace

FANNY J. CROSBY, 1820-1915

GEORGE C. STEBBINS, 1846-1945

1. Some day the sil - ver chord will break, And I no more as now shall sing;
2. Some day my earth - ly house will fall, I can-not tell how soon 'twill be,
3. Some day—till then I'll watch and wait, My lamp all trimm'd and burn - ing bright,

But, O, the joy when I shall wake With - in the pal - ace of the King!
But this I know— my All in All Has now a place in Heav'n for me.
That when my Sav - ior opes the gate, My soul to Him will take its flight.

CHORUS

And I shall see Him face to face,
shall see   to face
And tell the sto-ry—Sav'd by grace;

And I shall see Him face to face,
shall see   to face,
And tell the sto-ry—Sav'd by grace.

SINCE JESUS CAME INTO MY HEART

He brought me up also out of an horrible pit, out of the
miry clay, and set my feet upon a rock, and established my
goings. And he
hath put a new song in my mouth,
even praise unto our God.

—Psalm 40:2-3 KJV

It is always thrilling to hear or read the testimony of an individual whose life has been dramatically changed by a true spiritual conversion—hearing the truth of the gospel and responding in obedient faith.

The story is told of a widely known agnostic, Robert Ingersoll, challenging evangelist D. L. Moody to a debate regarding the validity of the Christian faith. Moody agreed on the condition that Ingersoll produce one person whose life had been transformed from degradation by the power of agnosticism. Moody in turn promised that he would produce innumerable individuals whose lives had been radically transformed by the power of Christ's gospel. Needless to say, the debate never took place.

The words for "Since Jesus Came into My Heart" were written in 1914 by a Disciples of Christ pastor, Rufus Henry McDaniel, following the death of his son. McDaniel stated that he wrote these words during this time of grief as a statement of his personal faith. Some time later the pastor attended one of the Billy Sunday-Homer Rodeheaver evangelistic campaigns and was awed by the many conversions and changed lives he witnessed. Following one of these services he showed his previously written lines to Charles Gabriel, the well-known song composer and publisher. In a short time Gabriel completed the vibrant music to match the words. He showed the manuscript to Homer Rodeheaver, who sang the new song at the next public meeting. The response was so great that it was necessary to print quickly thousands of copies for the next service. Moved by this testimonial gospel song, many individuals were converted to Christ during the following crusade meetings. This vigorous, energetic song about the gospel's transforming power is still a favorite with evangelical congregations.

For twenty years Billy Sunday and Homer Rodeheaver were teamed together in the most effective crusades conducted until that time. It is estimated that over one million individuals walked the "sawdust trail" to receive Christ. The impact of these meetings still lives on in the memory of those who were dramatically changed by the power of the gospel.

Express thanks that still today the vilest of sinners can be gloriously changed by the power of Christ's gospel.

For an inspiring collection of conversion stories, see *40 Fascinating Conversion Stories,* Samuel Fisk, comp. (Grand Rapids: Kregel Publications, 1993).

Since Jesus Came into My Heart

RUFUS H. McDANIEL, 1850-1940

CHARLES H. GABRIEL, 1856-1932

1. What a won-der-ful change in my life has been wrought Since Je - sus came
2. I have ceased from my wan-d'ring and go - ing a - stray, Since Je - sus came
3. I shall go there to dwell in that Cit - y, I know, Since Je - sus came

in - to my heart! I have light in my soul for which long I have sought,
in - to my heart! And my sins, which were man-y, are all washed a - way,
in - to my heart! And I'm hap - py, so hap - py, as on - ward I go,

CHORUS

Since Je - sus came in - to my heart! Since Je-sus came in-to my

heart, Since Je - sus came in - to my heart, Floods of joy o'er my

soul like the sea bil-lows roll, Since Je-sus came in-to my heart.

STAND UP, STAND UP FOR JESUS

Be on your guard; stand firm in the faith;
be men of courage; be strong.
Do everything in love.
                                        —1 Corinthians 16:13-14

"Tell them to stand up for Jesus."
These were the final words of a twenty-nine-year-old Episcopalian minister, Dudley Tyng, as he spoke from his deathbed to a group of sorrowing friends and fellow ministers.

A great citywide revival swept across Philadelphia in 1858. It was called "the work of God in Philadelphia." Of the participating ministers, none was more powerful than the Reverend Dudley Tyng, known as a bold and uncompromising preacher.

In addition to pastoring his own church, Tyng began holding noonday services at the downtown YMCA. Great crowds came to hear this dynamic young preacher. On Tuesday, March 30, 1858, over five thousand men gathered for a mass meeting to hear Tyng preach from the Exodus 10:11 text, "Go now ye that are men, and serve the LORD" (KJV). Over one thousand of these men committed their lives to Christ. At one point in the sermon the young preacher shouted, "I must tell my Master's errand, and I would rather that this right arm were amputated at the trunk than that I should come short of my duty to you in delivering God's message."

The following week, while visiting in the country and watching the operation of a corn threshing machine in a barn, the young pastor accidentally caught his loose sleeve between the cogs. His arm was lacerated severely, with the main artery severed and the median nerve injured. As a result of shock and a great loss of blood, Rev. Tyng died four days later.

On the following Sunday, Tyng's close friend and fellow worker, the Reverend George Duffield, pastor of the Temple Presbyterian Church in Philadelphia, prepared his morning sermon as a tribute to his departed friend. He chose Ephesians 6:14 (KJV) as his text:

> *Stand, therefore, having your loins girded about with truth, and having on the breastplate of righteousness.*

Pastor Duffield closed his sermon by reading a poem that he had just finished writing. He told his people that it had been inspired by the dying words of his esteemed friend. Soon the challenging words found their way into the hearts and hymnals of God's people around the world.

---

*Determine to "put on the whole armor of God"
(see Eph. 6:10-20) in the daily battle against the forces
of unrighteousness.*

*"Lift high his royal banner, it must not
suffer loss!"*

Stand Up, Stand Up for Jesus

THOMAS A. DORSEY, 1899-1993

GEORGE N. ALLEN, 1812-1877
Adapted by Thomas A. Dorsey

1. Stand up, stand up for Je - sus, Ye sol - diers of the cross!
2. Stand up, stand up for Je - sus, The trum - pet call o - bey;
3. Stand up, stand up for Je - sus, Stand in His strength a - lone;
4. Stand up, stand up for Je - sus, The strife will not be long;

Lift high His roy - al ban - ner— It must not suf - fer loss.
Forth to the might - y con - flict In this His glo - rious day.
The arm of flesh will fail you— Ye dare not trust your own.
This day the noise of bat - tle— The next, the vic - tor's song.

From vic - t'ry un - to vic - t'ry His ar - my shall He lead,
Ye that are men now serve Him A - gainst un - num-bered foes;
Put on the gos - pel ar - mor, Each piece put on with prayer;
To Him that o - ver - com - eth A crown of life shall be:

Till ev - 'ry foe is van - quished And Christ is Lord in - deed.
Let cour - age rise with dan - ger, And strength to strength op - pose.
Where du - ty calls, or dan - ger, Be nev - er want - ing there.
He with the King of glo - ry Shall reign e - ter - nal - ly.

SWEETER AS THE YEARS GO BY

_The righteous will flourish like a palm tree, they will grow
like a cedar of Lebanon; planted in the house of the LORD,
they will flourish in the courts of our God. They will still
bear fruit in old age, they will stay fresh and green,
proclaiming, "The LORD is upright; he is my Rock, and
there is no wickedness in him."_

—_Psalm 92:12-15_

For the believer, growing older should mean a greater awareness of God's love and fellowship as well as an increased desire for
usefulness in Christian service. The golden years should be the most fruitful time of life. A lifetime of companionship with God ought to produce a
more mellow and gracious Christlike spirit. Because there are fewer de-
mands and pressures in life, the older Christian can enjoy opportunities
for effective ministry that he or she has never attempted. A "do-nothing
retirement" must never become the goal of any believer's life.

There is nothing more tragic, however, than a professing Christian who
has grown disgruntled and self-centered in later years. It is true that as we
age we simply bring into full bloom the traits that were begun in our early
years. If, then, we wish to have positive and productive attitudes as seniors,
we must begin to develop these traits while we are still young.

This song's author and composer, Mrs. Lelia Naylor Morris, was an active worker in the Methodist church. She continued to write gospel songs

during the last fifteen years of her life, even after becoming blind in her early fifties. "Sweeter As the Years Go By" was written during the early years of her blindness. It is said that during this difficult time in her life, Mrs. Morris used a twenty-eight-foot-long blackboard with music lines to help her in writing hymns. She wrote more than one thousand hymn texts, as well as many of the tunes. She never stopped writing until the time of her home going.

Several of Lelia's other gospel hymns still in use include: "What If It Were Today?," "Let Jesus Come into Your Heart," and "Nearer, Still Nearer."

Mrs. Lelia N. Morris's handicap and age never deterred her from being productive for God. Despite the difficulties of life, she continued to "bear fruit" and to enjoy a relationship with her Lord that become sweeter with each passing year. What a worthy example for each of us to emulate!

---

*"With saints redeemed in glory, let us our voices raise,"
letting it be known with joy and conviction that our
relationship with the Lord becomes
"sweeter as the years go by."*

Sweeter As the Years Go By

MRS. C. H. MORRIS, 1862-1929

C. H. M.

THE OLD RUGGED CROSS

He himself bore our sins in his body on the tree, so that we might die to sins and live for righteousness; by his wounds you have been healed.

—1 Peter 2:24

This best known of all gospel songs was sold by George Bennard, then an unknown writer, to the Rodeheaver Music Company in 1913 for the grand sum of $25. The prophetic words of editor Charles Gabriel—"You will certainly hear from this song, Mr. Bennard"—were soon realized. "The Old Rugged Cross" became one of the most widely published songs, either sacred or secular, in this country. And still today it is continually ranked by the general public as the best-loved hymn. In jails and prisons throughout America it has become known as "the prisoner's anthem." Only eternity will reveal fully the number of lives that have been influenced for God by this one simply worded and easily sung gospel hymn.

George Bennard began his ministry as a young man with the Salvation Army. Bennard and his first wife served for a number of years as officers in this organization. The composer often stated that his experience with this ministry provided the inspiration which later led to the writing of "The Old Rugged Cross."

Although self-taught, Bennard was eventually ordained by the Methodist Episcopal Church, where his devoted service was highly esteemed for many years. He became involved in conducting revival meetings, especially throughout the states of Michigan and New York.

During this time Bennard passed through a particularly trying experience which caused him to reflect seriously on the significance of the cross and what the apostle Paul meant when he wrote in Philippians 3:10 of entering into "the fellowship of [Christ's] sufferings" (KJV). He stated:

> I saw the Christ of the cross as if I were seeing John 3:16 leave the printed page, take form and act out the message of redemption. The more I contemplated these truths the more convinced I became that the cross was far more than just a religious symbol but rather the very heart of the gospel.

On June 7, 1913, a choir of five members at a small church in Pokagon, Michigan, sang "The Old Rugged Cross" from a penciled copy of Bennard's manuscript. An "Old Rugged Cross Day" is still observed annually at this church, and on a large stone nearby are carved the names of the five original singers of the hymn and the significance of that memorable Sunday in 1913.

At the age of eighty-five, George Bennard exchanged his cross for a crown. At his home near Reed City, Michigan, stands a twelve-foot-high cross with these words: "The Old Rugged Cross—home of George Bennard, composer of this beloved hymn."

But God forbid that I should glory, save in the cross of
our Lord Jesus Christ.
—Galatians 6:14 KJV

The Old Rugged Cross

GEORGE BENNARD, 1873-1958

GEORGE BENNARD, 1873-1958

1. On a hill far a-way stood an old rug-ged cross, The em-blem of
2. O that old rug-ged cross, so de-spised by the world, Has a won-drous at -
3. In the old rug-ged cross, stained with blood so di-vine, A won - drous
4. To the old rug-ged cross I will ev-er be true, Its shame and re-

suf-f'ring and shame; And I love that old cross where the dear-est and best
trac-tion for me; For the dear Lamb of God left His glo-ry a-bove
beau-ty I see; For 'twas on that old cross Je-sus suf-fered and died
proach glad-ly bear; Then He'll call me some day to my home far a-way,

CHORUS

For a world of lost sin-ners was slain.
To bear it to dark Cal-va-ry. So I'll cher-ish the old rug-ged
To par-don and sanc-ti-fy me. cross, the
Where His glo-ry for-ev-er I'll share.

cross, Till my tro-phies at last I lay down; I will cling to the
old rug-ged cross,

old rug-ged cross, And ex-change it some day for a crown.
cross, the old rug-ged cross,

VICTORY IN JESUS

*In all these things we are more than conquerors through
him who loved us.*

—Romans 8:37

As believers in Christ, we are involved in a very real spiritual battle. We are engaged in a conflict in which many enemy strongholds must be conquered if we are to enjoy the abundant life of joy and victory. The Scriptures teach that our struggle is really "against the powers of this dark world and against the spiritual forces of evil in the heavenly realms" (Eph. 6:12). But the One who loved us enough to redeem our eternal souls and who provided the Holy Spirit to live within us makes it possible for us to be "more than conquerors."

Eugene Monroe Bartlett, Sr., author and composer of "Victory in Jesus," lived in the South, where he was known as a successful music teacher and publisher. He conducted singing schools throughout Arkansas and the surrounding states. His son, Eugene, Jr., trained under his father and later served as music director of several large Baptist churches before being appointed in 1954 to be Director of Church Music for the Baptist General Conference of Oklahoma. Both father and son have written a number of gospel songs, though none ever enjoyed the response of "Victory in Jesus," composed in 1939. Just two years after writing this song, Eugene, Sr., experienced his own prophetic words: "And some sweet day I'll sing up there the song of victory." The reassuring message and singable music have made this Southern-style gospel song a favorite with God's people everywhere.

The American singing school tradition as promoted by music teachers like Bartlett had a profound influence upon the development of gospel music. Many of the early gospel song leaders began their training in this way. The singing schools also strongly influenced congregational singing and the development of the nineteenth-century church music program in general.

The classes that trained students in sight reading and conducting were generally held at night in the country schoolhouses or churches. They were taught by a dedicated musician who traveled from place to place organizing and teaching laypeople to enjoy and use music in their local churches. The classes had a strong spiritual emphasis in addition to providing wholesome social activity for the community. These rural singing schools eventually evolved into the teacher-training normal schools in communities throughout our land.

———————————

God wants us to be victors, not victims; to grow, not grovel; to soar, not sink; to overcome, not to be overwhelmed.
—*William H. Ward*

Victory in Jesus

EUGENE M. BARTLETT SR., 1885-1941

EUGENE M. BARTLETT SR., 1885-1941

1. I heard an old, old sto - ry, how a Sav - ior came from glo - ry,
2. I heard a - bout His heal - ing, of His cleans-ing pow'r re - veal-ing,
3. I heard a - bout a man - sion He has built for me in glo - ry,

How He gave His life on Cal - va - ry to save a wretch like me;
How He made the lame to walk a - gain and caused the blind to see;
And I heard a - bout the streets of gold be - yond the crys - tal sea,

I heard a - bout His groan-ing, of His pre-cious blood's a - ton-ing,
And then I cried, "Dear Je - sus, come and heal my bro - ken spir - it,"
A - bout the an - gels sing - ing and the old re - demp - tion sto - ry—

Then I re - pent - ed of my sins and won the vic - to - ry.
And some - how Je - sus came and brought to me the vic - to - ry.
And some sweet day I'll sing up there the song of vic - to - ry.

CHORUS

O vic - to - ry in Je - sus, my Sav - ior, for - ev - er! He sought me and

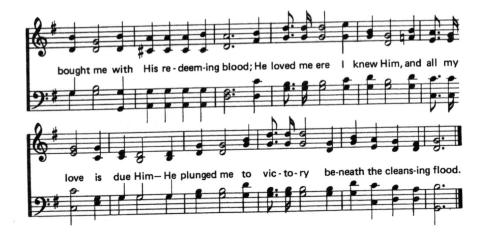

bought me with His re - deem-ing blood; He loved me ere   I   knew Him, and all my

love   is   due Him—He plunged me to   vic - to - ry   be-neath the cleans-ing flood.

WHAT A FRIEND WE HAVE IN JESUS

Do not be anxious about anything, but in everything, by prayer and petition, with thanksgiving, present your requests to God.

—Philippians 4:6

*P*erhaps no other hymn has ministered so much comfort and consolation as this simple but meaningful message of hope and cheer. As with many of our hymns, "What a Friend We Have in Jesus" was a result of much grief in the life of its author, Joseph Medlicott Scriven.

Joseph Scriven was born of prosperous parents in Dublin, Ireland, in 1820. At the age of twenty-five, Scriven suddenly decided to leave his native Ireland and migrate to Canada. His reasons for leaving seem to have been twofold: the spiritual influence of the Plymouth Brethren upon his life, which estranged him from his family; and the tragic death of his fiancée by accidental drowning on the evening before their scheduled wedding.

Upon arriving in Port Hope, Canada, Joseph Scriven began a totally different pattern of life. As the local school teacher and tutor, he gave himself completely to his students and the community. He took the Sermon on the Mount literally as his lifestyle. It is said that he gave freely of his limited possessions, even sharing the clothing from his own body when needed, and he never once refused help to anyone. He became known as a Good Samaritan throughout the area surrounding Port Hope.

Scriven never intended that "What a Friend We Have in Jesus" should be published. Ten years after he had said good-bye to his mother in Ireland, word came that she was seriously ill. Unable to return to his native land, Scriven wrote a letter of comfort to his mother and enclosed the words of his newly written poem with the prayer that these brief lines would always remind her of a never-failing heavenly Friend.

At the age of sixty-six, Joseph Scriven, like his fiancée, accidentally drowned. After his death the citizens of Port Hope erected a monument on which the entire hymn text is inscribed with these words added: "Four miles north in Pengally's Cemetery lies the philanthropist and author of this great masterpiece, written at Port Hope, 1857."

The music was added later by a very versatile American, Charles C. Converse, whose talents ranged from law to professional music. In 1875, Ira Sankey discovered the hymn just in time to include it in his well-known collection, *Sankey's Gospel Hymns Number One*. Later Sankey wrote, "The last hymn which went into the book became one of the first in favor."

If a person does not pray about everything, he/she will be worried about most things.

—author unknown

What a Friend We Have in Jesus

JOSEPH SCRIVEN, 1819-1886

CHARLES C. CONVERSE, 1832-1918

1. What a Friend we have in Je - sus, All our sins and griefs to bear!
2. Have we tri - als and temp-ta - tions? Is there trou-ble an - y - where?
3. Are we weak and heav-y - la - den, Cum-bered with a load of care?

What a priv - i - lege to car - ry Ev - 'ry-thing to God in prayer!
We should nev-er be dis - cour-aged— Take it to the Lord in prayer.
Pre - cious Sav-ior, still our ref - uge— Take it to the Lord in prayer.

O what peace we oft - en for - feit, O what need-less pain we bear,
Can we find a friend so faith - ful Who will all our sor-rows share?
Do thy friends de-spise, for - sake thee? Take it to the Lord in prayer;

All be - cause we do not car - ry Ev - 'ry-thing to God in prayer!
Je - sus knows our ev-'ry weak-ness— Take it to the Lord in prayer.
In His arms He'll take and shield thee— Thou wilt find a sol - ace there.

WHEN WE ALL GET TO HEAVEN

After that, we who are still alive and are left will be caught
up together with them in the clouds to meet the Lord in the
air. And so we will be with the Lord forever. Therefore
encourage each other with these words.
—1 Thessalonians 4:17-18

Learning to sing praise to God now is an excellent way of preparing ourselves for heaven. The Scriptures teach that praise and singing will be the believers' prime occupation throughout eternity. Someone has said, "Nobody dreams of music in hell, and nobody conceives of heaven without it." Allow your mind to anticipate that day in the heavenly courts when the entire family of God—those from every tribe, language, people, and nation—will see their Lord and together will "sing and shout the victory."

> This glorious hope revives our courage for the way,
> When each in expectation lives and longs to see the day
> When from sorrow, toil, pain, and sin, we shall be free,
> And perfect love and joy shall reign throughout all eternity.
> *—John Fawcett*

The author of this text, Eliza Edmunds Hewitt, was a school teacher in

Philadelphia and a Christian lay worker who was deeply devoted to the Sunday school movement. Like many of the other gospel song writers during the latter half of the nineteenth century, Eliza's goal in writing her songs was to reach children and teach them the basic truths of the gospel. She dedicated this particular song to her own Sunday school class in Philadelphia. Though an invalid for much of her life, Eliza was always active and enjoyed a long personal friendship with Fanny Crosby. These two women met often for fellowship and discussion of their new hymns. Eliza Hewitt wrote other gospel hymn texts such as "More About Jesus," "Stepping in the Light," and "There Is Sunshine in My Soul Today."

Miss Hewitt often attended the Methodist camp meetings at Ocean Grove, New Jersey. It was here that she collaborated with Emily Wilson, the wife of a Methodist district superintendent in Philadelphia, in the writing of this triumphant gospel hymn—a favorite of young and old alike. "When We All Get to Heaven" was first published in 1898.

The anticipation of heaven has often been described as the oxygen of the human soul. "Everyone who has this hope in him purifies himself, just as he is pure" (1 John 3:3).

When by His grace I shall look on His face,
That will be glory, be glory for me.

—Charles H. Gabriel

Allow this glorious hope to brighten each day and keep you "true, faithful, trusting, serving . . ."

When We All Get to Heaven

ELIZA E. HEWITT, 1851-1920

EMILY D. WILSON, 1865-1942

1. Sing the won-drous love of Je - sus, Sing His mer - cy and His grace;
2. While we walk the pil - grim path-way Clouds will o - ver - spread the sky;
3. Let us then be true and faith-ful, Trust - ing, serv - ing ev - 'ry day;
4. On - ward to the prize be - fore us! Soon His beau - ty we'll be - hold;

In the man - sions bright and bless - ed He'll pre - pare for us a place.
But when trav - 'ling days are o - ver Not a shad - ow, not a sigh.
Just one glimpse of Him in glo - ry Will the toils of life re - pay.
Soon the pearl - y gates will o - pen— We shall tread the streets of gold.

CHORUS

When we all get to heav - en, What a day of re-
When we all What a

joic - ing that will be! When we all see
day of re - joic - ing that will be! When we all

Je - sus, We'll sing and shout the vic - to - ry.
shout, and shout the vic - to - ry.

WONDERFUL GRACE
OF JESUS

*For you know the grace of our Lord Jesus Christ, that
though he was rich, yet for your sakes he became poor, so
that you through his poverty might become rich.*
—2 Corinthians 8:9

The Scriptures have much to teach us about the importance
of God's grace in our behalf. Ephesians 1:7 states that Christians are
to *enjoy the riches of His grace*. Second Peter 3:18 challenges us to *grow
in grace*. Colossians 3:16 instructs us that we are to *sing with grace*.
Colossians 4:6 reminds us that *our speech should always be with grace*.
And the writer of the book of Hebrews encourages us to approach the
throne of grace with confidence in order to *find grace to help in time of
need* (4:16).

This inspiring gospel hymn about the grace of God was written in 1918
by one of the important twentieth-century gospel hymn writers and publishers, Haldor Lillenas.

It was while pastoring the Church of the Nazarene at Auburn, Illinois, between 1916 and 1919 that Lillenas wrote the text and music for "Wonderful
Grace of Jesus." He left the following account:

In 1917, Mrs. Lillenas and I built our first little home in the town
of Olivet, Illinois. Upon its completion, we had scarcely any
money left to furnish the little home. Having no piano at the time,

and needing an instrument of some kind, I managed to find at one of the neighbor's home a little wheezy organ, which I purchased for $5.00. With the aid of this instrument, a number of my songs were written which are now popular, including "Wonderful Grace of Jesus." It was sung by the great chorus, in 1918, at the Northfield, Massachusetts, Bible Conference, being introduced for the first time by Homer Hammontree.

Several years later the song was published in the *Tabernacle Choir Book,* for which Lillenas was paid the grand sum of $5. The hymn soon became popular around the world with both choirs and congregations.

Haldor Lillenas wrote approximately four thousand gospel hymn texts and tunes. In addition to "Wonderful Grace of Jesus," other Lillenas songs still widely sung by congregations include "The Bible Stands Like a Rock Undaunted," "It Is Glory Just to Walk with Him," "Jesus Has Lifted Me," and "My Wonderful Lord." Before his home going on August 18, 1959, Lillenas was recognized for his many accomplishments in the gospel music field and was awarded an honorary Doctor of Music degree from Olivet Nazarene College in Kankakee, Illinois.

May these words by Haldor Lillenas be our joyous response to God for His wonderful gift of grace:

*O magnify the precious name of Jesus,
praise His name!*

Wonderful Grace of Jesus

HALDOR LILLENAS, 1885-1959

HALDOR LILLENAS, 1885-1959

1. Won-der-ful grace of Je - sus, Great-er than all my sin;
2. Won-der-ful grace of Je - sus, Reach-ing to all the lost,
3. Won-der-ful grace of Je - sus, Reach-ing the most de - filed,

How shall my tongue de-scribe it, Where shall its praise be - gin?
By it I have been par-doned, Saved to the ut - ter - most;
By its trans-form-ing pow - er Mak - ing him God's dear child,

Tak - ing a-way my bur - den, Set - ting my spir - it free,
Chains have been torn a - sun - der, Giv - ing me lib - er - ty,
Pur - chas-ing peace and heav - en For all e - ter - ni - ty—

For the won - der-ful grace of Je - sus reach - es me.
For the won - der-ful grace of Je - sus reach - es me.
And the won - der-ful grace of Je - sus reach - es me.

CHORUS

Won - der-ful the match-less grace of Je - sus,
the match-less grace of Je - sus,
Deep-er than the